Pioneer
Free Will Baptists
Ministers
Burial Locations
In
Texas

PIONEER FREE WILL BAPTISTS MINISTERS BURIAL LOCATIONS IN TEXAS

This book was printed in the United States of America.

To order additional copies of this book, contact:
FWB Publications
Enchanting Acres
1006 Rayme Drive
Columbus, Ohio 43207
Alton.loveless@prodigy.net
Or
www.amazon.com

FWB
FWB Publications

Introduction

Texas

This book represents all that were part of the Free Will Baptist movement, consisting of the Palmer (south), Randall (north) and others such as the Stone, John-Thomas, John Wheeler Assns., NC OFWB and more.

Many of the photos are poor quality, but it was all I could find. Likewise, I do not have photos or tombstones for many of them. The information about these ministers were all that was available to me or found in archives. I made every effort to include those for which they would be remembered. Some I had no information, but research had shown they were of our denomination.

This Section is taken for a two Volume set done by this author.

Texas

Rev. Gladys E. Beam
Birth:
Oct. 16, 1904
Death:
Jan. 14, 1996
Burial:
Edom Cemetery
Edom
Van Zandt County
Texas

She was the wife of Grady W. Beam (1904 - 1932).

Hubert Ray Berry, Jr
Birth:
Nov. 10, 1943
Houston, Harris County,Texas
Death: Jun. 9, 2014
Hoover, Shelby County,Alabama
Burial:
Neeley Cemetery
Pone, Rusk County,Texas

H. Ray Berry, Jr. of Hoover, AL, was born to the late Rev. H. Ray, Sr. and Asa Hillin Berry. Ray graduated from Bryan High School in 1960 and Old Dominion University in 1973. He pastored several churches and founded Christian Deaf Fellowship. He was a source of joy and encouragement to everyone he met.

Hubert Ray Berry, Sr
Birth:
May 26, 1912
Death:
Burial:
Jul. 2, 1999
Neeley Cemetery
Pone, Rusk County, Texas,
Plot: R 1 F 4

Well Known Texas pastor and church builder. His son: Hubert Ray Berry (1943 - 2014) is buried in Texas and a daughter is married to FWB pastor Dale Burden.

Alan Jackson Birdwell
Birth:
Apr. 14, 1881
Death:
Oct. 17, 1932
Burial:
Myrtle Springs Cemetery
Myrtle Springs
Van Zandt County, Texas

Early Texas minister.
Father's Name: W E Birdwell
Mother's Name: Alice Flanigan

Joseph Leeford Bounds
Birth: 1887
Death: 1940
Burial:
Oak Hill Cemetery
Edgewood
Van Zandt County
Texas, USA

Spouse: Helen Brown Bounds (1896 - 1943)*
Children: Leeford Gayther Bounds (1918 - 1978)*

Lewis K Brashier
Birth:
Sep. 26, 1905
Death:
Feb. 13, 1990
Burial:

Stewart Cemetery
Henderson
Rusk County
Texas,

Parents: James Plinie Brashier (1873 - 1928)- Lillie Curry Brashier (1873 - 1951)

Spouse: Clover Brashier (1909 - 1980)

Children: James Lewis Brashier (1926 - 2001)

Siblings: Coey Lee Brashier (1893 - 1949)- Lucile Brashier Jacks (1897 - 1988)- Wilburn Arling Brashier (1902 - 1956)- Lizzie Mae Brashier Harrison (1905 - 1988)- Lewis K Brashier (1905 - 1990)

John Andrews Brooks
Birth:
Jun. 6, 1893
Death:
Feb. 24, 1973
Clay County,
Texas
Burial:

Pleasant Valley Cemetery
Buffalo Springs
Texas

Brooks was born on June 9, 1893, in Gravette, Arkansas. He migrated to Texas with his family and in 1912 he married Edith Covington, sister of Rev. Tiff Covington. John and Edith had ten children. John was ordained to the gospel ministry on August 14, 1917, by the West Fork District Association of Free Will Baptists. In the 1920's he attended one semester at Decatur Baptist College in Decatur, Texas.

John Brooks had a long and distinguished ministry. He pastored about a dozen churches, all of them in the West Fork Association. He founded the First Free Will Baptist Church of Wichita Falls, Texas, in 1952. Preaching revival meetings took him to Oklahoma and New Mexico occasionally.

During the many years of his ministry he worked at manual labor to support himself and his large family, and never pastored a church full-time. Early in his ministry he moved his family to West Texas to work in the cotton fields which seemed to extend to the horizon. In the late 1930's John and his brother-in-law, Tiff Covington, held a six weeks long revival meeting in a brush arbor at Buffalo Springs, Texas. At the end of the revival they baptized one hundred twenty converts in a stock tank. In other states a stock tank would be called a pond. During World War II there were not enough Free Will Baptist preachers for all of the small, rural churches to each have a pastor. During this time he pastored four churches at once, preaching at each of them one Sunday per month. He was widely admired as being an effective preacher and he was called upon frequently to speak at district and state meetings in Texas. He retired from active ministry at the age of seventy-six. He passed away on February 24, 1973. His beloved wife Edith passed away on September 22, 1985, at the age of ninety-five

Rev James Cary Caraway
BIRTH

14 Oct 1871
Hardin County, Texas, USA
DEATH
20 Sep 1956 (aged 84)
Liberty County, Texas, USA
BURIAL
Franks Branch Cemetery
Fred, Tyler County, Texas

Early minister in Texas

Stephen Monroe Carter
BIRTH
1854
Mississippi, USA
DEATH
20 Mar 1934 (aged 79–80)
Waples, Hood County, Texas, USA
BURIAL
Acton Cemetery
Acton, Hood County, Texas

He was the son of Steve Carter who was born in North Carolina and Mollie (Adama) Carter who was born in South Carolina. He was mar to Minerva (unk) CARTER. An Eld. S.M. Carter, Granbury, Hood Co. TX

registered as a minister in a 1912 meeting of the Southwestern Co-op Ass'n of Free Will Baptists. He gave his residence as Granbury, Hood Co. This appears to be him, even though the census says his occupation was 'farmer', most old ministers farmed to make a living as they recv'd little in ministry work, and they didn't consider it an occ., but a calling.

William Thomas Franklin "Tom" Clement
Birth: Mar. 12, 1869
Death: Jun. 10, 1947
Burial: Greenleaf Cemetery Brownwood, Brown County, Texas,

Parents: Peter Richard Clement (1840 - 1914) Wife: Sarah Isabell Reed(Read) Clement (1848 1891) Children: Thomas Ezra Clement (1893 - 1894)

John David Cole
Birth: Nov. 26, 1867
Parker County
Texas, USA
Death: Nov. 27, 1935
Millsap
Parker County
Texas, USA
Burial:
Cole Cemetery
Corner
Parker County
Texas, USA

Son of George W. and Elizabeth Boatman Cole. Married Margaret "Maggie" Lena Millsap June 17, 1888 in Parker Co., TX. Father of Lottie, Eula, Jackie, and Martin Leonodus Cole.

Parents:
George W Cole (1843 - 1917)
Elizabeth Boatman Cole (1846 - 1894)

Rev J G Cole
Birth:
Jun. 19, 1866
Death:
Jun. 4, 1917
Burial:
Balch-Senterwood Cemetery
Alvarado
Johnson County, Texas

Jasper Wilburn Cook
Birth:
May 28, 1915
Death:
Feb. 23, 2007
Burial:
Oakwood Cemetery
Cisco, Eastland County, Texas
Plot: Block 247, Lot 5, Space 5

Jasper Wilburn Cook, 91, of Cisco, Texas. Jasper attended five colleges and universities. From a comedian in Vaudeville he became a successful pastor. His preaching, music and singing, as well as his poetry, reveal his love for mankind and his desire to help his fellow man. He had a zest for life and will be sadly missed.

William Henry Coonrod
BIRTH
7 Jan 1884
Fannin County, Texas, USA
DEATH
9 Sep 1962 (aged 78)
Bonham, Fannin County, Texas, USA
BURIAL
Cedarlawn Memorial Park
Sherman, Grayson County, Texas

Wm. Henry Coonrod, was the son of John and Elizabeth (Smithee) Coonrod. Occupation was a retired minister. His name appears in 1929 Minutes of the Center Ass'n of Free Will Baptists, in Pontotoc Co. Okla, as living at Davis, OK which was included in their district. Interesting, a John W. Smithey, a minister and member whose family was from Grayson/Bonham area was also living at Davis, OK. (Note that Wm. H's mother m/n was "Smithee" on TX d/cert). In the 1940 and 1941, meetings, he gave his address as Burris City, OK, where he is listed as pastor. In the 1944 list of pastors, it gives his address as Dennison, TX.

H, Zirl Cox
Birth:
November 30, 1919
Antelope, Texas
Death:
1993
Duncanville,
Dallas County, Texas
Burial:
Vashti Cemetery, Vashti,
Clay County, Texas
Harry Zirl Cox was born to Robert Ebbie and Margaret Sue (Blackmon) Cox. He was licensed to

the gospel ministry in 1941. He earned a Bachelor's degree in Bible from Dallas Baptist College and in 1953 he earned a Master of Theology degree from Bible Baptist Seminary. He served in the United States Army during World War II as a medic and chaplain's assistant from 1943 to 1945. During the last year of the war he served in Germany as the Allied Army closed in on Berlin and destroyed Hitler's plans for a thousand year empire. H. Z., as he was commonly known, married Artelle Barnette and they had three children: Robert, Michael, and Cynthia Ann. His first pastorate was the New Salem Free Will Baptist Church, just south of Decatur, Texas, which he pastored from 1945 to 1947. In September of 1947 he became pastor of the First Free Will Baptist Church of Dallas, Texas, and embarked on a long and productive ministry which would make him well known, not only in Texas, but in the denomination at large. He became a full-time pastor in 1954 and continued as pastor of the First Free Will Baptist Church in Dallas until his retirement in November of 1986, thirty nine years. The church changed locations and built new facilities on several occasions due to the steady growth of the church. His final move was to the Dallas suburb of Duncanville, at which time the church became the First Free Will Baptist Church of Duncanville. Brother Cox was a skilled businessman and located the church on prime, highly visible property in a rapidly growing community. The church building is beautiful and expansive.

Brother Cox served as moderator of the West Fork District Association for a number of years, as he did for the Texas State Association of Free Will Baptists. He served a term on the National Home Missions Church-Extension Board, and was very active in home missions in Texas, on both a district and state level. His business acumen was utilized in numerous projects in the state. He had a knack for getting things done. He represented Texas as a delegate to the meeting in Nashville, Tennessee, when delegates from each state association met to hammer out a workable agreement on the question of the state of the backslider. The statement upon which they agreed was inserted as an appendix into the *Free Will Baptist Treatise* in July of 1969.

One of his loves was the West Fork Youth Camp. He worked in the camp faithfully every year until his health no longer pemitted it. He served in many capacities at the camp, but he perhaps is best known for taking the campers on a morning hike and devotion time.

The conference room in the Barber Center at Hillsdale Free Will Baptist College in Moore, Oklahoma, is named the H. Z. Cox Conference Room because of his support of the college.

Rev Tiff Covington
Birth:
Aug. 25, 1895
Panola, Kentucky
Death:
Nov. 3, 1984
Burial:
Buffalo Springs Cemetery
Buffalo Springs (Clay County)
Clay County, Texas

Anderson Tifton "Tiff" Covington was born to Milton Conner and Charlotte Covington. The Covington family, parents and ten children, migrated to Clay County, Texas, arriving in Henrietta by train on September 3, 1908. Tiff was thirteen years old at the time. They settled in the Buffalo Springs community. In August of 1916 Tiff was converted at a revival meeting being conducted in the Pleasant Valley community by Rev. J. W. Shults, and was baptized in a nearby stock tank. He married the daughter of Rev. Shults, Carrye Dell, on July 29, 1917. Carrye was always called Carrye D to distinguish her from Tiff's sister Carrye. Their first home was a ten by twelve foot tent, with a dirt floor. It was furnished with a bed, cook stove, cabinet, and a trunk. From this marriage came four children: Granvel, Marverene, Wilburn Conner, and Ramona.

In 1918 Tiff was drafted and reported to Henrietta to be inducted into the army. The head of the draft board told him, "Tiff, you're not going because you are needed more at home." His father was an invalid by this time. The head of the draft board took Tiff to Dallas that day and got him released from his military obligation.

Though he only had a seventh grade education, Tiff answered the call to the ministry and was licensed to preach in 1928. Shortly thereafter he became the pastor of the New Salem Free Will Baptist Church in Decatur, Texas. He was also called to be the pastor of the Pleasant Valley Will Baptist Church, south of Buffalo Springs. He was ordained by the West Fork District Association in 1932, at the Silver Creek Free Will Baptist Church near Azle. In 1936 the Pleasant Valley church relocated and changed its name to the Pleasant Mound Free Will Baptist Church, widely known as The Rock Church. For several years Tiff pastored both the New Salem and the Pleasant Mound churches, preaching at New Salem once a month.

During the early years of his ministry he worked as a carpenter and farmer to support his family, because the churches could not pay him a livable salary. Tiff and Ruel Conner organized the First Free Will Baptist Church in Bowie, Texas, and Tiff pastored it for seven years. Carrye D had a series of strokes and became bedridden. Tiff moved to Wichita Falls so she could be near the doctors. He became the pastor of the First Free Will Baptist Church in Wichita Falls, pastoring it for nine and a half years. Carrye D passed away on February 12, 1962. Tiff then married Ethel Inman on January 1, 1963.

In 1967 Tiff once again became pastor of the Pleasant Mound Free Will Baptist Church at Buffalo Springs and pastored there until May 1, 1980.

Over the years Tiff became a legend in North Central Texas, not so much because of his pastoring, but because of the funerals he conducted. He had a gift for it. He spoke with such compassion, empathy, and sweetness that people far and wide wanted Tiff Covington to preach their funerals. During his lifetime he conducted well over three thousand funerals. He preached some very productive revival meetings. One such meeting was begun by Rev. M. L. Sutton at Buffalo Springs, who preached for two weeks, morning and evening. Then Tiff and a

Methodist minister continued it, taking turn's morning and night. Tiff finished the meeting, which altogether lasted for thirty-one days. There were eighty-two conversions and rededications.

Another revival meeting in Buffalo Springs was conducted by Tiff and his brother-in-law, Rev. John A. Brooks. After the six weeks revival they baptized one hundred twenty converts in a stock tank.

Tiff was a popular preacher and spoke many times at quarterly meetings and state association meetings. He pastored a total of fifty-two years, all of them in the West Fork District Association.

Rev. Jasper Creamer
Birth:
Jul. 24, 1852
Georgia
Death:
Dec. 21, 1925
Plainview
Hale County,Texas
Burial:
Indian Creek Cemetery
Comanche
Comanche County,Texas

The Creamers lived in Alabama until October, 1869, when they moved to Texas. After living one year on the Brazos River, they moved to Comanche County, where they farmed and were proprietors of a store in the Creamer Community. They traveled extensively to preach at many churches. The December 7, 1923, Comanche Chief Newspaper carried a front page announcement of Jasper's death, in which it stated: "A minister of the gospel of the Freewill Baptist persuasion, for more than fifty years he had carried the story of Jesus through the pioneer country. Traveling horseback, in a buggy, and often on foot, he was faithful in the discharge of his duty....Earth has one pure spirit less, heaven one pure soul more."

Parents: Abraham K. Steele (1813 - 1884)- Elizabeth Caroline Malone Steele (1830 - 1901). She was married to Rev. Jasper Clinton Creamer (1843 - 1923).

Martha Jane Steele Creamer
BIRTH
24 Jul 1852
Georgia, USA
DEATH   21
Dec 1925 (aged 73)
Plainview, Hale County, Texas,
BURIAL
Indian Creek Cemetery
Comanche, Comanche County,
Texas

Mrs. Creamer is listed in the 1909 and 1911 Free Will Baptist Register as being a member of the Salt Springs Free Will Baptist Church in Comanche, member of the West Texas Association and member of the Southwestern Free Will Baptist General Convention. She is listed as a licensed minister in the minutes of the 1912 Southwestern Convention.

Wm. H. Davidson
Birth:
1859
Death:
1943

Burial:
Restland Memorial Park
Dallas
Dallas County
Texas
Plot: Section H

Rev. Z B Dally
Birth:
Mar. 12, 1870
Death:
Mar. 24, 1958
Burial:
Algoma Cemetery
South and North
Marshall
Harrison County
Texas
Plot: Section:
Center Circle

He who has gone,
so we but cherish his
memory, abides with us,
more potent, nay,
more present than the
living man.

Rev William H "Bill" Denmon
Birth:
Jul. 23, 1860
Texas
Death:
Sep. 28, 1923
Burial:
Denman Cemetery
Jasper County
Texas

Kirby Chapman
Birth:
Jul. 23, 1896
Death:
Sep. 22, 1973
Burial:
Leagueville Cemetery
Leagueville
Henderson County
Texas, USA
Plot: Row 17 # 37

He was pastor of the Bryan First FWB in 1919-1920.

From the Southeast Texas Freewill Baptist Association minutes at Friendship Church, Jasper County, Texas on Thursday night before the second Sunday in October 1923.

It has pleased an All-Wise Creator to remove from out midst Bro. W. H. Denmon, who was a minister of the Gospel from the 13th day of October, 1905 until his death, who departed this life September 28th, 1923.

Bro. Denman leaves a wife and seven children, with a host of friends to mourn their loss. But we trust that our loss is his eternal gain.
Rev. Wm. Henry Denmon attended the SoWest Coop. Association in 1910, in TX, and gave his residence

as "Buma." He listed his occ. as 'farmer' on most censuses, as that was the means of their support; preaching/ministering was a "calling" and not counted on census.

William D Denman
Birth: Mar. 17, 1906
Death: Mar. 19, 1966
Burial:
Antioch Cemetery
Buna
Jasper County
Texas

Parents: Amon and Nancy Denman

Joseph S. Dillard
Birth: Jun. 20, 1856
Alabama
Death: Apr. 5, 1932
Alabama City
Etowah County
Alabama

Burial:
Waxahachie City Cemetery
Waxahachie
Ellis County, Texas

Rev. J. S. Dillard was living in Ellis Co 1910 census with his wife & children, and his widowed son-in-law's Buse family. His name was listed in the 1912 Minutes in a roll of ministers and he listed Italy, Ellis Co.

Daniel W Diserens
Birth:
Sep. 1, 1894
Death:
Mar. 10, 1979
Burial:
Masonic Cemetery
Gatesville
Coryell County
Texas
Parents:
John William Diserens (1872 - 1971)
Mary E Shehorn Diserens (1872 - 1906)
Spouse:
Minnie M Diserens (1895 - 1971)*
Siblings:
Daniel W Diserens (1894 - 1979)
Lillie E Diserens (1896 - 1907)**

Wesley Alvin Diserens (1898 - 1981)*

Mary Diserens (1906 - 1907)**

Walter F. Diserens (1913 - 2003)**

Kittie Bowen Diserens Jerome (1916 - 2004)**

Flora Troy Diserens Potter (1918 - 2005)

Rev Devan Judson Dollar
Birth:
Mar. 2, 1854
Alabama
Death:
Nov. 7, 1931
Rusk County
Texas
Burial:
Mount Hope Cemetery
Joinerville
Rusk County
Texas

Parents: John A Dollar & Martha Ann Nutt Dollar. A minister in the New Hope Association of Free Will Baptists, in 1899 in Arkansas.

Spouse:
Amanda Melvina Alford Dollar (1854 - 1924)*

Rev James William Doster
BIRTH
30 Jun 1863
Alabama, USA
DEATH
22 Jun 1932 (aged 68)
BURIAL
Newburn Cemetery
Center, Shelby County, Texas

Early Free Will Baptist minister in Texas

James Hill Dowell
Birth:
Jan. 28, 1882
Willowhole, Madison County, Texas
Death:
Mar. 29, 1953
Kerrville
Kerr County
Texas
Burial:
Willowhole Cemetery
North Zulch
Madison County, Texas

James Hill Dowell was married to Miss Nancy Batson in 1901. He united with the Baptist Church early in life and was ordained as minister of the gospel by Free Will Baptist Church in 1911. He spent 22 years in pastoring churches. Services were conducted by Rev. J. D. Walker assisted by Rev. A. R. Housewright and Rev. McDonald of North Zulch. Married Nanie Batson 17 Nov 1901 in Madison Co., TX

Hezekiah C. Dunn
BIRTH
12 Apr 1854
Georgia, USA
DEATH
13 Jun 1931 (aged 77)
Henderson,
Rusk County, Texas,
BURIAL
New Prospect Cemetery
New Prospect,
Rusk County, Texas

H. C. Dunn was in a roll of ministers in 1912, of SW Coop Association of Free Will Baptists, listing his address as Henderson, TX.

Robert Burnett Easley
Birth:
Sep. 1, 1850
War Eagle
Benton County, Arkansas
Death:
Dec. 26, 1940
Vandyke
Comanche County, Texas
Burial:
Zion Hill Cemetery
Comanche
Comanche County, Texas

He was the second son of Burnett M. and Orpha Dorinda (Garrett) Easley. He married Mary Ann McGuire on January 22, 1870, in Benton County, Arkansas. The following year, 1871, he migrated to Comanche County, Texas. He founded the Easley's Chapel Free Will Baptist Church, just north of

Comanche, Texas, when he was thirty-six years old. The church was founded in his pasture, across a creek, upon a hill, south of his home, under an old fashioned brush arbor.

The congregation met in several different places at first. In the 1870's, when Comanche County was pretty much on the western edge of the Texas frontier, with bands of Comanches still roaming free in West Texas, people came from far and near to attend Easley's Chapel, especially for revival meetings and singings.

Then, in 1889, they built a church building. The lumber for the building was hauled from Dublin, Texas, by team and wagon. The church was constructed by Rev. Easley, the deacons, and church members.

In 1935 three acres of land were purchased from Mrs. J. E. Gartman, where the church is presently located. Pastor Easley said, "We will call this place Gartman's View." That's why some call the church Easley's Chapel and others call it Gartman's View.

Rev. Easley was the father of eleven children: John M., Zora, Thomas, Orpha D., Dicie, Simon Peter, Deffa, Robert Burnett, Jr., Phillip Jeff, William Paul, and Luke Ellery Easley. Many of his descendants still live in the Comanche-DeLeon area. The Easley Chapel Church continues its ministry well into the twenty-first century.

Rev. R. B. Easley, as he was known, was one of the true pioneers of the Free Will Baptist work in Texas. As other Free Will Baptist churches were started nearby, Easley's Chapel became a member of the West Texas Free Will Baptist Association, which was organized in 1891. Later the Easley's Chapel Church joined the West Fork Association, of which it is still a member. In 1910 or 11, while attending a Free Will Baptist convention near Tecumseh, Oklahoma, Rev. Easley met a young, licensed woman preacher by the name of Miss Elizabeth Lawless, whom he brought to Comanche to pastor the Easley Chapel Church until the spring of 1911. That young woman would later become well known as Rev. Mrs. Lizzie McAdams. Pastor Easley was a mentor and an encouragement to other young preachers, as well. His name is still spoken with veneration and admiration in the area where he lived and ministered.

Rev John A Edmonson

Birth:

Jul. 25, 1865

Death:

Jul. 10, 1940

Burial:

Eastview Memorial Park

Vernon

Wilbarger County

Texas,

Plot: 12-8-5

His name was in a minister's roll in Minutes of the Southwest Cooperative Association of Free Will Baptists in 1910. Spouse: Ella Mosely Edmonson (1867 - 1938)

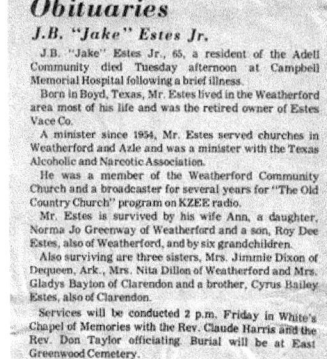

James Bailey Estes, Jr

Birth: Mar. 13, 1914

Texas,

Death: May 15, 1979

Weatherford

Parker County

Texas,

Burial:

East Greenwood Cemetery

Weatherford

Parker County, Texas

Parents: James Bailey Estes (1885 - 1965)- Margaret Lelia Cross Estes (1889 - 1971)

Spouse:- Annie Marie Hardin Estes (1917 1999)

Clifford Mabry Fain

Birth:
Dec. 14, 1879
Death:
Dec. 14, 1967
Burial:
Prairie View Cemetery
Aransas Pass
San Patricio County
Texas

Clifford M. Fain

Clifford M. Fain; 88, of 3050 Sunnybrook, died at 3:45 a.m. today in a local nursing home after a long illness.

A resident of Ingleside from 1929 to 1964, Fain was retired from Humble Oil and Refining Co. He moved to Corpus Christi three years ago.

Funeral services will be at 2 p.m. tomorrow at the First Baptist Church in Ingleside with the Rev. W. A. Butler, a retired minister, officiating. Burial will be in Prairie View Cemetery in Aransas Pass under direction of Cage-Mills Funeral Home here.

Surviving are four sons, L. R. Fain of Corpus Christi, W. T. Fain of LaPorte, T. A. Fain of Baytown and W. L. Fain of Pampa; 11 grandchildren, and nine great-grandchildren.

s/o Thomas Fain
Spouse:
Eula Eugenia Smith Fain (1883 - 1961)*
Children:
Loy R Fain (1905 - 1983)*
Ethel Faith Fain (1909 - 1911)*
Thomas A Fain (1914 - 1992)*
Welton Leon Fain (1915 - 1999)*

Johnny Lee Fears

Birth:
Aug. 1, 1906
Death:
Dec. 7, 1975
Burial:
Neeley Cemetery
Pone
Rusk County
Texas Plot: R 5 B3
Retired minister in the Free Will Bapt churches in his area.

Spouse: Lou Mary Weems Fears (1916 - 2009)
Children: Gwindolyn Rae Fears Chapman (1929 - 2015)- Dan Gregory Fears (1939 - 1991)- Betsy Dean Fears (1940 - 1940)

A. F. Ferguson

Birth:
Nov. 8, 1909
Memphis,
Shelby County, Tennessee
Death:
Apr. 18, 2008
Georgetown,
Williamson County, Texas
Burial:
Tyler Memorial Park & Cemetery,
Tyler, Smith County, Texas

Allie Fennel Record Ferguson was born in Memphis, Tennessee, on November 8, 1909.

When he was yet a boy his father moved the family by train to Alvarado, Texas. After World War I the family moved to Berryvillle, Arkansas. There Allie attended a school named Hide Out. Allie became a Christian at the age of sixteen, while they still lived in Arkansas. The family made several moves and then ended up at Sherman, Texas.

Jessie Zeona Van was born near Gainesville, Texas, on September 17, 1912. She became a Christian in June of 1925. A new family moved to the community and all of the teenage girls were in a buzz about the handsome new boy. It had been Jessie's prayer for some time that she would marry a preacher and be a preacher's wife. Word got around that the good looking young man was going to be a preacher. It was almost too much to believe that this fellow would become her husband. She almost dismissed the idea. She thought he didn't know she existed. Unknown to her he was praying about who would be his life's partner. In church their eyes met and there was an instant attraction. Her beautiful eyes and sweet smile kept drawing his eyes to hers. She Couldn't keep her eyes off him. Eighteen months later they went to Durant, Oklahoma, and were married on Sunday afternoon, November 29, 1931. In time Allie

and Jessie had two children, Norman and Glenna.

During the Great Depression of the 1930's work was hard to find for an unskilled laborer.

He tried in Oklahoma, Missouri, and Arkansas. Allie and Jessie moved to Fort Worth where Allie found a job with Justin Boot and Shoe Manufacturers. The day he went to work he had one dime in his pocket. He worked a fifty-four hour week for a salary of $9.00. With his paycheck he had to support seven mouths, because Allie and Jessie lived with his mother and siblings.

Allie and Jessie attended the First Free Will Baptist Church, then the Trinity Free Will Baptist Church, both pastored by Rev. M. L. Sutton, who became their mentor. In 1931 Allie was licensed to the gospel ministry by the West Fork District Association and then ordained in August of 1933. His peers were men such as Tiff Covington, Ruel E. Conner, and Bill McPhail. H. Z. Cox and Clarence Hearron were two of his younger peers. Jessie also answered the call to preach and she was licensed by the West Fork on September 1, 1934. She was ordained to the gospel ministry on January 27, 1946.

His first pastorate was the New Hope Free Will Baptist Church in Parker County. Over the next half century Allie pastored sixteen churches in Texas, California, Oklahoma, and Mississippi, always willing to go wherever God in His providence took him and Jessie.

While pastoring the Shafter Church in California Allie served on the Board of Trustees of California Christian College.

Allie and Jessie started the Bible Free Will Baptist Church in Odessa, Texas, which he pastored for eight years. At the peak of their ministry in Odessa the church attendance ran in the 60's and 70's.

During his ministry in Weatherford, Texas, the house was full, with a great many young people attending.

Jessie never pastored, but did preach. Her work was mostly assisting Allie in his ministry and raising a family. She was a leader in the Woman's Auxiliary work in Texas.

During more than sixty years in the gospel ministry Allie pastored 16 churches. He and Jessie were always active in the district and state work, especially in Texas. He preached on many occasions at district and state meetings, and very often was part of a spontaneously formed quartet which provided special music for the meetings. He and H. Z. Cox were two of the men who helped organize and have the first summer youth camp in the West Fork District Association.

On the occasion of Allie's 93rd birthday,

Dr. Jack Williams, editor of Contact Magazine, wrote:

Thank God for the A. F. Ferguson's
Who broke the ground...

Laid the foundation...
Planted the crop...
worked in the shadows...
and let guys like me stand on their
shoulders.

Rev. Mrs. Jessie Ferguson

Jessie passed away on March 24, 1993. Allie's home going occurred on April 18, 2008.

Allie and Jessie are buried in the Tyler Memorial Cemetery in Tyler, Texas. Graveside services for the Rev. A.F. Ferguson, 98, Georgetown, were held with the Rev. James Walker officiating. He was born to the late Thomas and Jeannie Ferguson. He pastored 16 churches and started two over a period of 60 years in Texas, Oklahoma, Mississippi and California. He was a member of Lake Hills Freewill Baptist Church of Cedar Park, and a junior founder of Justin Boot Co. in Fort Worth. He was preceded in death by his wife of 62 years, Jessie Ferguson. Published in the *Tyler Morning Telegraph* on 4/21/2008.

Lewis Franklin Fitzgerald
Birth:
May 22, 1893
Johnson County, Texas
Death:
Sep. 20, 1955
Vernon
Wilbarger County
Texas, USA
Burial:
Eastview Memorial Park
Vernon
Wilbarger County, Texas

He was an early minister in the area. His name appears in a conference of Free Will Baptists, Southwestern Cooperative Association, in 1912, with residence Tama, Coryell Co. TX. Son of John Fitsgerald and Lorenda (Baker) Fitzgerald. Spouse: Allie Shepherd, Mar. 1914, Wilbarger Co. TX.

James Alexander Ford
Birth:
Jul. 14, 1842
Death:
Oct. 24, 1912
Burial:
Pleasant Grove Cemetery #01
Decatur,
Wise County, Texas

Rev Josephus Wesley Ford
Birth:
Jan. 31, 1848
Death:
Jul. 19, 1898
Burial:
Pleasant Grove Cemetery #01
Decatur, Wise County, Texas

Rev. Josephus Wesley Ford and Markley Stanford "Sandy" Ford married sisters, Eliza Ann Young and Lurana Elizabeth "Luraney" Young. And their brother, Rev. William Henry Ford, Sr., married the aunt, Elizabeth E. "Bet" Young, of these Young sisters. In the McDonald County records, page 633, dated August 15, 1880: *"This certifies that the bearer, J. W. Ford, of the County of McDonald and State of Missouri a regular member of the Free Will Baptist Church in said county has this day been publicly set apart to the work of the gospel ministry by prayer and laying on of hands according to the usage of the Freewill Baptist Denomination and is hereby authorized to preach the Gospel and administer its ordinances whenever God in his providence may call him."* Rev L H Robertson, ordaining M H Ford, council This August the 15th 1880. Filed and recorded May 4 1887. John Black, clerk "*Goodspeed's* 1888 History of McDonald & Newton Counties shows the Free-Will Baptist Church of Gooden Hollow as organized in September, 1886, at the Wilson Mill, with J.W. Ford as moderator. The membership in March, 1888 was nineteen, with Rev. J. W. Ford, preacher. The Western Mount Zion quarterly meeting convened July 8, 1887 with the Pleasant Hill Free-Will Baptist Church, on White Rock Prairie, with a delegation from eight churches, and seven ministers. Rev. J. W. Ford officiated as moderator. Free-will Baptist Churches were located at Oak Grove, Pleasant Hill, Hopewell, Gooden Springs, Wire Springs, Sulphur Springs, McDonald County Church, Antioch Church, & Shiloh Church. Rev. Josephus Wesley Ford was one of the organizers of the New Salem Free Will Baptist Church on 4 Apr 1893 at the old Perrin School House near Decatur, Wise County, Texas. According to family history from the family of his son 'Pate' Ford, he died at the 'dinner on the grounds' after running a 'foot race' and taking a big bite of fresh honey. From Josephus's son Roy's daughter, Goldie Mae Wood in Dodge City, Kansas a partial copy of his obituary: (the first part was missing-)............in the beautiful home of the soul. To the bereaved family and church' the beautiful sentiments of the poem comes as a welcome greeting in his hour and we too will" Judge not the Lord by feeble sense. But trust him for his grace, behind a frowning providence He shows a shining face." A Freewill Baptist himself, Bro. Ford came from a race of Free wills and Methodists and his warm friendship came from the fact that he recognized God's children in all churches. He was born in Washington County, Arkansas, in 1848. He has been in the ministry 18 years; was married in 1871 to Miss Eliza Ann Young, and to them were born 13 children, 12 of whom are now living and 5 of whom are now trying to meet their father in that happy land. It is hard to realize that our (at this place the newspaper clipping had deteriorated) _ _ _ _ _ r (father?), our friend, and our pastor beyond is in an unknown land. To all our inquiries the still small voice replies, do your duty to God to yourself and to your fellowman and leave the rest to Him who doeth all things well. He is gone from among us and a grateful church mourns his loss and honors his memory. The church tenders its heartfelt sympathy to her whose sorrow is the deepest and to the bereaved family. We gently fold the drapery of his couch about him and lay him down to sleep where immortals and forget-me-nots will bloom over his grave. We try to bow with resignation to the summons that called him away. And we leave him with the angels who will stand by his tomb and keep watch over his slumbers; and we invoke Him who is above all angel's principalities and powers, to care for her whom his dispensation has left widowed and alone in the world. The life boat soon is coming by the eye of faith I see. As she sweeps through the waters to rescue you and me. She will land us safely in the port with the friends we love so dear. Get ready cries the captain. Oh look! She is almost here.John T. Sanford, Josephus Wesley Ford was also a member of the Masonic Lodge in Wise County, Texas, and after his death, his widow was heard to say she could not have raised her family without the help of the Masons. They wrote: In Memorium: Whereas it has pleased the All wise and Supreme Ruler of the Universe to call from our midst our beloved brother Rev. J. W. Ford who departed this life July 18, 1898. Again the Golden Chain has been broken and we bow submissing to his will believing that our loss is his gain and that our worthy brother has been called to refreshment in that Celestial Lodge above where the Supreme Architect presides. Therefore be it resolved that Azle Lodge #60I A.F. and A. M. Azle Texas has lost a zealous member, his church a faithful worker, his family a loving husband, and kind father, and the community a good man, and neighbor. Resolved that these resolutions be spread upon our minutes, and copies be furnished the widow of our deceased brother, and the Decatur and Fort Worth papers for publication. Gladden Lovell, J. W. Walker, Com.J. Frank Snodgrass.- Larry Carpenter

Rev Markley Stanford Ford
Birth:
Mar. 25, 1852
Newton County
Missouri
Death:
Feb. 12, 1917
Wise County
Texas
Burial:
Fairview Cemetery
Midland
Midland County
Texas

Rev. Markley Stanford "Sandy" Ford and Rev. Josephus Wesley Ford married sisters, Lurana Elizabeth "Luraney" Young and Eliza Ann Young and their brother Rev. William Henry Ford, Sr., married the aunt, Elizabeth "Bet" Young, of these sisters.

For those who love history, there were often family members who told the stories that lay behind the photographs, and family.

Sandy Ford is No More

Markley S. Ford, a citizen of Decatur since 1893, died at his home Monday morning in North Decatur. He was 65 years old. The burial took place at the Fairview cemetery, south of town, the services being conducted by Rev. Moreland. A number of friends and relatives attended the funeral. "Sandy" as he was known to all our people, will be missed. He was a good man; honest as the day was long, and true as steel to his God. Fate had been unkind to this man; he strived and battled against adversity; he contested the cruel advance of poverty for many long years, and, although a mere shadow of a physical man, he fought heroically. Through it all he smiled and battled the best he could, feeling assured that the rest coming after the storm on this earth would last for countless ages. "Sandy" Ford's spirit went home to his God; he stood the acid test, a test that has made multiplied millions lose hope and grope in the gloom of despair, and his reward has come. Man more brilliant than he have shuffled off this mortal coil; kings of finance, postmasters of art and literature have answered the roll call that calls before this world, who not one for the last time with greater assurance of a real and beyond the stars than my friend, Sandy Ford.

Tommie Franklin
Birth:
Feb. 19, 1896
Bryan
Brazos County, Texas
Death:
Aug. 7, 1977
Bryan
Brazos County, Texas
Burial:
Bryan City Cemetery
Bryan
Brazos County, Texas
Block 6, Lot 25, Space 1.

Tommie Franklin was born in Brazos County, Texas, in 1897. Some of the earliest Free Will Baptist churches in Texas were in that area of Central Texas. On one rainy Sunday morning when Lizzie McAdams was a guest preacher at the First Free Will Baptist Church in Bryan,

Tommie (Pictured top left with Ava Walker and Rev's Hiram and Lizzie McAdams) pastored several churches during her ministry: one in Washington, North Carolina, the First Free Will Baptist Church of Denison, Texas, the First Free Will Baptist Church in Bryan, Texas, a Free Will Baptist church near Henderson, Texas, and the Parkview Free Will Baptist Church in Desloge, Missouri.

Tommie met her for the first time. The young Miss Franklin confided in Lizzie that she had been called to preach, but felt that ministry was closed to her. Over lunch the two women had a heart to heart talk about the possibility of Miss Franklin entering the ministry. The next day Tommie joined Lizzie in Mexia, Texas, and went with her to Tecumseh, Oklahoma, where Lizzie dropped her off to attend Tecumseh College, a Free Will Baptist school, for Bible training. When the summer break came Tommie went to North Carolina and became a member of Lizzie's evangelistic team. She would be a member of that team, on and off, for several years.

Tommie was of a sweet disposition and gentle smile and was committed to the Lord all of her life. She was listed as one of the ordained ministers in the Central Texas District Association until her death, but in those latter years was not active in the ministry as the idea of women preachers was falling into disfavor, even though Free Will Baptists had a long heritage of them dating back to 1790.

Her simple, flat, marble headstone reads only "Tommie Franklin 1897-1977." Tommie's funeral was conducted by Dr. Eugene Richards.

Rickey Lynn Futch
BIRTH
26 Jan 1958
Henderson, Rusk County, Texas,
DEATH
6 Oct 2002 (aged 44)
Bryan, Brazos County, Texas, USA
BURIAL
Rusk County Memorial Gardens
Henderson, Rusk County, Texas

Zachary T Fuller
Birth:
1848
Death:
1929
Burial:
North Belton Cemetery
Belton
Bell County
Texas
Plot: 569 Old Section

He was in the roll of ministers in 1912 at the session of the Southwestern Co-op Association of Free Will Baptists. His D/C states he was a minister, and it gave the title "Rev." in front of his name.

James C. Gartman
Birth:
Dec. 27, 1885
Youngsport
Bell County
Texas, USA
Death:
Mar. 31, 1952
Burial:
Sharp Cemetery
Killeen, Bell County, Texas

He was a young lad when his father died; his mother carried on, as censuses show. A strong family. Parents:

Rev Thomas E. Glaze
Birth:
Nov. 15, 1858
Limestone County
Alabama, USA
Death:
Oct. 31, 1929
Burial:
Abilene Municipal Cemetery
Abilene
Taylor County
Texas, USA
Plot: Masonic 3/7/10

An early Free Will Bapt. minister in Texas, his name appearing in Minutes of the Southwestern Cooperative Association of FWB in 1912. He listed his residence as Haskell, TX

Barney A Grant
Birth:
Apr. 28, 1902
Death:
Dec. 26, 1997
Burial:
Lakewood Memorial Park
Henderson
Rusk County, Texas

Rev John E Graham
Birth:
Jan. 3, 1866
Coryell County
Texas
Death:
Dec. 23, 1948
Gatesville
Coryell County
Texas
Burial:
Restland Cemetery
Gatesville
Coryell County
Texas

Rev. John E. Graham, born in the Harmony Community, was a son of Curtis Beason Graham and Elizabeth Jane Thornton Graham. Rev. John E. Graham married Nancy Elizabeth "Betty" Brookshire. They had four children.

Rev Walton Graham
Birth:
Aug. 28, 1868
Texas, USA
Death:
Feb. 7, 1941
Rylie
Dallas County

Texas, USA
Burial:
Kleberg Cemetery
Kleberg
Dallas County
Texas, USA

Clyde Forrest Goen
Birth:
Apr. 26, 1893
Death:
Feb. 9, 1985
Burial:
Bright Light Cemetery
Bryan, Brazos County,Texas
Inscription:
U.S. Navy WWI

Rev Barney Atlas Grant
BIRTH
28 Apr 1902
Texas, USA
DEATH
26 Dec 1997 (aged 95)
Gladewater,
Upshur County,
Texas, USA
BURIAL
Lakewood Memorial Park
Henderson,
Rusk County,
Texas

Andrew Martin Griffin
BIRTH
22 Feb 1867
Tennessee, USA
DEATH
16 Jun 1962 (aged 95)
Fort Worth, Tarrant County, Texas,
USA
BURIAL
Venus Cemetery
Venus, Johnson County, Texas,

Parents: Palace Griffin and Martha (unk) Griffin. He was m. to Martha/Mattie Hamilton, 20 Aug. 1885, Lincoln, Tenn.

Dolphus Crawford Hargrove
Birth:
Nov. 5, 1868
Hopkins County, Texas
Death:
Sep. 8, 1946
Navasota
Grimes County,
Texas
Burial:
Zion Methodist Cemetery
Iola
Grimes County,
Texas

HARGROVE was born to James William Hargrove and Dorinda E. Couch. Dolphus was first married on 27 Nov 1889 to Anna Ophelia Gressett in Grimes County, Texas, and they had FOUR His first wife passed away on 16 December 1899.

Dolphus second marriage was on 11 January 1905 to Anna Artelia Young in Grimes County, Texas.

Dolphus passed at Brazos Valley Hospital in Navesota.

The Central Texas District Association, formed in 1906, sent Rev. John Swanwick and Rev. D. C. Hargrover as delegates to the Southwestern Convention in 1908.

Hubert Haskel Haston
Birth:
Mar. 4, 1898
Oklahoma, USA
Death:
Mar. 22, 1981
Paducah, Cottle County, Texas
Burial:
Garden of Memories Cemetery
Paducah, Cottle County, Texas

Spouse: Eunice Naomi Burleson Haston (1899 – 1974), Children: David Elmer Haston (1921 – 1944), Clark W. Haston (1927 – 2014), Rachel Ann Haston Cole (1938 – 2013).

Rev John C Harvey
BIRTH
2 Sep 1855
Tennessee, USA
DEATH
10 Jun 1932 (aged 76)
Waco, McLennan County, Texas,
BURIAL
Rosemound Cemetery
Waco, McLennan County, Texas,
PLOT   Section O 49

W D Haston
Birth:
May 10, 1860
Death:
Jun. 4, 1929
Burial:
Buck Creek Cemetery,
Paducah, Cottle County, Texas

At about 30 years of age, he entered the ministry and affiliated with the Free Will Baptists. He married Sallie McLemore, 16 Sept. 1880, Yell Co. AR. He and Sallie later moved to Texas and continued in work and raising a large family.

A short notice/bio of his death appeared in the Free Will Baptist paper, *"The Gem"* July 1929 issue, in Missouri, where Eld. J. A. Edmondson, wrote that he was called to conduct his fellow minister's funeral in Paducah, TX. He stated Eld. W.D. Haston "had for over 40 years, preached all over and organized churches."

For those who love history, there were often family members who told the stories that lay behind the photographs, and family.

Alvin Floyd Halbrook
Birth:
May 27, 1914
Womack, Missouri
Death:
Jul. 23, 2000
Bryan
Brazos County, Texas
Burial:
Bryan City Cemetery
Bryan
Brazos County, Texas

He began pastoring even before he was licensed to preach. He pastored the Richwood's Free Will Baptist Church and others from 1933 to 1939. He was licensed to preach on July 31, 1936, by the St. Francois County Quarterly Conference of Free Will Baptists. He was ordained by them in 1938. One of the names on his ordination certificate is illegible, but the names of the other people who signed it are Elder James F. Miller, of Flat River, and Elder Tommie Franklin of Desloge. Alvin realized the need for specific training for the ministry and enrolled at Free Will Baptist Bible College, and began classes in 1944. There he met Miss Ida Frances Tinnin of North Carolina. While in Nashville he served as interim pastor of the East Nashville Free Will Baptist Church, one of the denomination's foremost churches in the 1930's and 40's.

Alvin finished his schooling at the Bible College and graduated, in 1945, as did his future wife, the aforementioned Miss Ida Frances Tinnin. Alvin and Ida were married on July 7, 1945, in Durham, North Carolina.

In August of 1945 Alvin Ida moved to Texas. For the next several years he pastored several Texas churches on a rotating basis. These included the North Zulch Free Will Baptist Church, the Evergreen Free Will Baptist Church, the Blue Lake Free Will Baptist Church, and the Bright Light Free Will Baptist Church. In 1947 Bright Light built a parsonage so the Halbrooks could live and serve near the church, and they moved there. He continued to preach on Saturday and Sunday afternoons at churches which did not have a pastor for almost all of his time at Bright Light.

Alvin never pastored a church full-time, always having to work at a secular job to support his family. During his tenure at Bright Light he worked in the library at Texas A&M University.

He was graduated from A&M in 1955. He wrote his thesis on rural churches.

He was a studious sort of person, and that's what enabled him to be a teaching pastor. He loved to study God's Word and memorize Scripture. Even in his older years he studied and read continually. The Lord was both his passion and his hobby. He loved people, too. It was his practice to carry a little notepad in his pocket and whenever he met people, he would write their names in it so he could remember them and pray for them.

Alvin held a number of positions in the Central Texas District Association: assistant clerk, ordaining council, credentials committee, foreign missions board, and moderator. Her served for several years as clerk of the Texas State Association of Free Will Baptists, beginning in 1950, served on the Superannuation Board and served on the Texas Foreign Missions Board.

He retired from Bright Light in 1968. He then worked at the Bryan Municipal Golf Course. During his retirement years he pastored the North Zulch Free Will Baptist Church, though he continued working at a secular job.

Alvin passed away on July 23, 2000. Ida then passed away on April 5, 2006.

Julia Keener Harper
Birth:
Jul. 7, 1873
Death:
Jan. 6, 1944
Burial:
Grace Hill Cemetery
Longview
Gregg County, Texas

Julia Keener was born July 7, 1873, to Nancy Matilda Brown and Jesse A. Keener of North Carolina. She married William M. Harper (1871-1956) and they had 7 children, including Ira Harper, who was also a Free Will Baptist minister in East Texas. The minutes of the four-teenth annual session of the Texas Free Will Baptist Convention, which met at the Woodlawn Church in McClelland, County, August 28-31, 1928, has a partial list of the ministers in the association. Listed as one of the ministers of the association is Mrs. Julia Harper, Route 2, Marshall, Texas. She is also listed in the 1929 minutes as living at Route 2, Marshall. Daughter of Jesse Keener

and Nancy Matilda Brown (Madison, NC)

Everett D. Hellard
Birth:
Sep. 29, 1923
Death:
Feb. 11, 2007
Texas
Burial:
Garden Park Cemetery,
Conroe,
Montgomery County, Texas

He pastored churches in many areas for the Free Will Baptist and was a leader at all levels. His beautiful tenor voice caused him to have many invitations to sing at many of the conventions. *Ship Ahoy* was always asked as the song for him to sing.

Rev Robert Elias Helms
Birth: Nov., 1854
Tennessee
Death: Jan. 20, 1930
Wichita County
Texas
Burial:
Riverside Cemetery
Wichita Falls
Wichita County
Texas

Plot: Block C, lot 3, sp 5
Parents: John F. Helms (1820 - 1897). Spouse: Amy Frances Coleman Helms (1859 - 1947)
Children:
John Critton Helms (1876 - 1959)*
Annie Elizabeth Helms Joyner (1879 - 1955)*
William Jennings Helms (1888 - 1964)*
Robert D Helms (1895 - 1974)*

Rev Lemuel Herrin
Birth
:   1787
Death:
Aug. 25, 1852
Burial:
Old Macedonia Cemetery
Holland Quarters
Panola County
Texas
Spouse: Mary   Hendon   Herrin (1787 - ____)
Children: Elizabeth   Herrin Scruggs   (1820   -   1870)- Karenhappuck   Herrin   Winder (1826 - 1892)-   Lorenzo   Herrin (1835 - ____)*

Rev William Jackson Higgins

Birth: Feb. 2, 1862
Prentiss County
Mississippi, USA
Death: Aug. 4, 1944
Stephenville
Erath County
Texas
Burial:
West End Cemetery
Stephenville
Erath County
Texas

He was born in Prentice Co., MS, and died in Stephenville, Erath Co., TX. He married Sarah Paralee Harty on 12 September 1880, in Young Co., TX.

Rev J. C. Hodges

Birth: Mar. 15, 1860
Death: Dec. 20, 1944
Burial:
Greenwood Memorial Park and
Mausoleum
Fort Worth
Tarrant County
Texas, USA

William Matthew Higgins

Birth:
May 3, 1883
Young County
Texas
Death:
Apr. 8, 1916
Floyd County
Texas
Burial:
Lakeview Cemetery
Floyd County, Texas

John Burton Holmes

Birth:
1850
Death:
1925
Burial:
Bethel Methodist Church
Cemetery
Parker County
Texas

Rev J B Hooser
Birth:
1857
Death:
1922
Burial:
Girard Cemetery
Girard
Kent County
Texas

Children:
Eugene G. Hooser (1891 - 1976)*
Joseph Fletcher Hooser (1895 - 1965)*

Egbert Statewright Jameson
Birth:
Oct. 16, 1878
Rusk County,
Texas
Death:
Feb. 25, 1950
Henderson,
Rusk County,
Texas
Burial:
Tatum Cemetery
Tatum,
Rusk County; Texas

Egbert Statewright Jameson was the son of D. R. Jameson of Alabama & Mary Irwin of Texas. His occupation was a Minister.

Rev. Jameson became a minister (from his obit) about 1905, and presumably ordained about that time. He was affiliated with the Free Will Baptist, and in the 1915 Convention of the Southwestern Convention, held at Stratford, OK (Garvin Co. OK) was the elected President of that Convention. This Convention was formulated about 1901 of Missouri, Oklahoma and Texas churches that had not merged in the northeastern Randall FWB movement with the Northern Baptists in 1911.

He was also a school teacher in Rusk Co. TX.

--taken from book by Rev. G.W. Million, pub. 1958, "A History of Free Will Baptists."

Rev D. R. Jimmerson
Birth:
May 14, 1853
Death:
Jul. 4, 1934
Burial:
Crow Cemetery
Henderson
Rusk County
Texas, USA

Minister of the Free Will Baptist church, b. AL. His name is in the Minutes of the Southwestern Cooperative Association of FWB in 1910.

Minnie L Jimmerson
Birth:
Jul. 27, 1892
Death:
Feb. 26, 1935
Burial:
Crow Cemetery
Henderson,
Rusk County, Texas

J. W. Johnson
Birth:
Aug. 4, 1845
Death:
Jul. 24, 1899
Burial:
King Cemetery
Henderson County, Texas

In1888 he was one of the ministers in the Denton Creek Association of Free Will Baptist which is located northwest of Dallas.

Inscription:
Co K3 Texas Cav C.S.A.

Billy Marion Jones
Birth:
Feb. 3, 1937
Houston Harris County Texas
Dec. 19, 2011
Fort Smith
Sebastian County, Arkansas
Burial:
Steep Hollow Cemetery,
Bryan,Brazos County, Texas

Bill was a minister, pastor, missionary to Ivory Coast for 10 years, editor of *"Heartbeat"* a missions magazine in Nashville, TN, President of Hillsdale Free Will Baptist College in Moore, OK for 8 years, Director of Oklahoma Missions for 2 years, served on the Foreign Mission Board for 26 years, professor of Theology at the college, Senior Adult pastor Poteau FWB Church.

Rev J. E. Jones
Birth:
Jul. 4, 1809
Death:
Dec. 20, 1876
Burial:
Rutland Cemetery
Douglassville
Cass County,Texas

Inscription:
Born in Abbeville Dist. S. C.
Died in Atlanta, Texas

Rev Mrs Amanda Jane Crouse Kester
Birth:
Jan. 20, 1891
Miami
Ottawa County, Oklahoma
Death:
Apr. 5, 1957
Henderson
Rusk County, Texas
Burial:
Lakewood Memorial Park
Henderson
Rusk County, Texas

Daughter of Henry Crouse and Emma Majors, both born Oklahoma.She was a housewife, 66 years old, widowed, and a resident of Henderson for the past 3 years. Informant was Mrs. Eva Dobson; burial was April 7, 1957. Pearson Funeral Home was in charge of arrangements.
(Texas death certificate# 22146)
Spouse: Charles Joseph Kester (1880 - 1946)

Inscription:
Mother
Have Faith In God

Joshua Timothy "Tim" Lee
Birth:
May 6, 1859
Decatur County
Georgia,
Death:
Apr. 16, 1931
Kirbyville
Jasper County
Texas
Burial:
Kirbyville City Cemetery
Kirbyville
Jasper County, Texas

Husband of Emily Ann Westbrook Lee. Father of 12 children, all of Kirbyville,TX. Son of Elias M.C.Lee and Dorcus Morgan Lee, Georgia.

Rev Jay Truron Lee
Birth:
Feb. 2, 1912
Death:
Jan. 22, 1982

Burial:
Gann Cemetery
Lufkin
Angelina County, Texas

Spouse: Wruble Wilson Lee (1920 - 2011)

J W Loftis
Birth:
Nov. 8, 1869
Death:
Jan. 8, 1906
Burial:
Jacksonville City Cemetery
Jacksonville
Cherokee County,
Texas

He was one that the earlier pastors in the Brazos Quarterly Meeting which was started in 1887.

James Pierce "Jim" Lunsford
Birth:
1834
Tennessee
Death:
Nov. 27, 1918
Burial:
Old Prospect Cemetery
Mount Enterprise
Rusk County
Texas

James Pierce Lunsford was born to Aris and Mary Lunsford, who had come from South Carolina. James married Sarah Ann Walters of Georgia, in Chattahoochee County, Georgia, on June 27, 1855. James and Sarah Ann moved to Covington County, Alabama, about 1862.

James was a Confederate soldier in the American Civil War, serving between 1862 and 1865. He served in the First Alabama Heavy Artillery Battalion, Company D, and fought in the Battle of Mobile Bay and the Battle of Spanish Fort. The Battle of Spanish Fort took place from March 27 to April 8, 1865 in Baldwin County, Alabama, as part of the Mobile Campaign of the Western Theater of the war. He was wounded, captured, and then released at the end of the war.

His family came to Texas in a wagon train after the Civil War, about 1876, and settled in Cherokee County. Later they lived in Rusk County where he started the Old Prospect and Mount Union Free Will Baptist churches.

When James founded the Old Prospect Church in Rusk County

1887, it was started in a building shared with the Methodists. The original building still stands beside the newer Baptist church next to it. There is a petrified wood marker by it.

James and Sarah Ann raised eleven children, two of them being born in Texas. Sarah Ann, died in 1908. Both are buried in the Old Prospect Cemetery. His grave spot in the cemetery is unknown, but many other relatives are buried there, presumably beside him.

James Thomas Lynch
BIRTH
26 Jan 1873
DEATH
5 Aug 1947 (aged 74)
BURIAL
Itasca Cemetery
Itasca, Hill County, Texas, USA
PLOT   I5

Isaac Martin
Birth:
Dec. 31, 1812
Death:
Nov. 2, 1888
Burial:
Alto City Cemetery
Alto
Cherokee County
Texas

He was one of the early ministers in Chattahoochee Association in Georgia and is recorded in the 1842 minutes. He married Mary Polly Truitt on June 6, 1834 in Jasper County, Georgia. She died in 1890 in Cherokee County, TX; Reverend and Mrs. Martin had eleven children. His parents were James Martin (1788 – 1869) and Hester Bogan Martin (1789 – 1867) who is buried in Georgia and was the parents of four preachers one of which started the Martin Association in the state of Georgia. Isaac is a brother to Samuel C. Martin listed below along with Rev. George W. Martin buried in Georgia and Rev. Robert Martin buried in Louisiana.

Rev John Andrew Martin

Birth:
Feb. 16, 1852
Death:
Apr. 5, 1932
Burial:
Mann Cemetery
Colmesneil
Tyler County
Texas

Parents: Wiley Martin (1829 - 1882)- Mary Ann Sears Martin (1832 - 1910)
Spouse: Elizabeth Enloe Martin (1854 - 1898).

Inscription:
A faithful soldier of the cross

Robert Martin

Birth:
Aug. 24, 1856
Death:
Jun. 23, 1871
Burial:
Steep Hollow Cemetery
Bryan
Brazos County
Texas
Plot: Section 2, Space 281

An early minister in Texas Parents: Samuel Crawford Martin (1825 - 1903) Sarah Ann Cheshire Martin (1824 - 1901)

Elder Samuel Crawford Martin

Birth:
Jan. 20, 1825
Alabama
Death:
Dec. 23, 1903
Steep Hollow
Brazos County, Texas
Burial:
Steep Hollow Cemetery
Bryan
Brazos County, Texas
Plot: Section 2, Space 278

Transcription of Obituary from The Bryan Eagle, Thursday, 24 Dec. 1903. REV. S. C. MARTIN DEAD. Venerable Pioneer Baptist Preacher Gone to his Reward. Brazos county mourns the loss of one of her oldest, noblest and best citizens, and the holidays have been darkened in homes throughout the length and breadth of the county, where his name was a household word, by the death of Rev. S. C. Martin at his home in the Steep Hollow community on Wednesday morning, December 23, 1903, at 8:30 o'clock. Rev. Martin, infirm with the weight and labors of 79 years, has been in failing health for some time and ill for several weeks, so that his death was not unexpected. Nevertheless, it was a sad blow to the family and host of friends when the news came from the darkened chamber that his noble spirit had taken its flight. Rev. Martin was a native of Alabama and came to Texas before the civil war, locating in Tyler County. He moved to Brazos County more than thirty years ago and has since resided in the Steep Hollow community. For more than half a century he preached the gospel and his labors were graciously blessed in the salvation of soul. Not only did he serve as pastor of nearly every Baptist church in Brazos County, but though out his life he did much successful revival work. He was sincere, earnest, uncompromising, unselfish and consecrated. He labored as faithfully without reward as when his labors were abundantly rewarded. In deed his best service was given to the Master with numerically weak and struggling churches, and it may be truly said that he gave his life to the gospel, the church and humanity.

His brother was the founder of the Martin Association in the state of Georgia and had three other brothers who were Free Will Baptist preachers. His ancestry has roots in South Carolina with one of them buried in the Horse Branch Free Will Baptist Cemetery. I am strongly assuming that he was also a Free Will Baptist preacher even though I have not been able to find verification of that in the state of Texas.

Elizabeth R McAdams
Birth:
Oct. 1, 1884
Luverne,
Alabama
Death:
Sep. 1, 1964
Burial:
Falba Cemetery,
Huntsville,
Walker County,
Texas

At 13 she recalls she wanted to be a missionary. At 25 she felt that God was calling her to preach. She was licensed to preach in October, 1910. In 1911 she married Rev. Hiram McAdams and they established themselves as an evangelistic team in North Carolina, Missouri, Texas, Oklahoma, Arkansas etc. Elizabeth became known as Lizzie, or Sister Lizzie, realized her teenage dream of being a missionary when she, her husband, and 6 year old Naomi Rebecca went to Barbados, British West Indies, in 1918 as missionaries. They spent a short time on the island and then returned to the States as evangelists. Back in the States Mrs. McAdams worked hard at trying to bring Free Will Baptist in the West and East together. At the meeting in Cofer's Chapel in 1935, she stood and made the motion that East and West unite as the National Association of Free Will Baptists, and without a reading of the committee's report on the Treatise, the motion passed and the National Association became a reality. At her death at the age of 80, she had spent 54 years in the ministry. In her book, *Rolling Stones,* she summed up her ministry: "We have preached in 17 states, have held about 300 revivals with about 10,000 professions of faith in the Lord Jesus, organized 11 churches and numerous Auxiliaries and Leagues in different states. During this period of time, spent four years as home missionaries. She also wrote *My Experiences, Six Gospel Sermons, Rolling Stones, Go Tell that Fox, Getting a Shave in the Devil's Barbershop, My Trip to the West India Islands,* and *Woman's Bible Right to Preach the Gospel.* She was also a member of the national home mission board in the early years of the denomination. She was active in travieIng among our churches. She was an evangelist, a promotional Secretary for various departments, and was pastor of a number of churches.

Hiram Mullens McAdams
Birth:
Jun. 18, 1879,
Walker County, Texas,
May 24, 1964
Huntsville,
Walker County, Texas,
Burial:
Falba Cemetery, Huntsville,
Walker County, Texas

McAdams married Elizabeth Rachel Lawlis, in 1911.They had a daughter, Naomi R., in 1913, born in Texas. Rev. Hiram and his wife, Rev. "Lizzie" as she was affectionately called, were ordained as ministers in the 1920's in the Free Will Baptist Church. They were co-pastors, and an evangelistic team holding large revivals in North Carolina, Texas, Alabama, Oklahoma, Missouri, and Nebraska. They organized churches and promoted Tecumseh College in Oklahoma, and was active in church missions throughout. In 1918, they acquired passports and went to Barbados,

West Indies, as missionaries for a short time, before they returned to become very involved in mission work in the states. His wife wrote several books, some of which described their work. They were respected and held in esteem by those who knew them, and in memory by those who read and know of their labors. It is noteworthy that Rev. "Lizzy" outlived her husband only three months and 8 days.

Elder Thomas J McBride
Birth:
1851
Death:
1913
Burial:
Bright Star Cemetery
Wills Point
Van Zandt County
Texas

An ordained Free Will Baptist minister, his name appearing in roll of ministers in 1910 Minutes of Southwest Cooperative Association of FWB, including states of Missouri, Oklahoma and Texas.

Spouse:
Minerva A Kinard McBride (1859 - 1904)

Children:
Mittie C McBride Furrh (1884 - 1970)*
Ella Mable McBride Rusk (1889 - 1959)*
Henry George McBride (1891 - 1976)*

Rev Thaddeus James McBride
Birth:
Feb. 13, 1909
Tuttle
Grady County
Oklahoma
Death:
Mar. 23, 1986
Paige
Bastrop County
Texas
Burial:
McBride Family Cemetery
Paige
Bastrop County
Texas, USA
Plot: Private Land

Married Martha Reed in Mena, Arkansas on March 26, 1937. Parents: Hiram Young McBride (1857 - 1937)-Lovica Colbert McBride (1868 - 1963)

John Henry Measures
Birth:
Oct. 27, 1901
Texas
Death:
Jun. 26, 1978
Parker County
Texas
Burial:
Memory Gardens of the Valley
Weatherford
Parker County
Texas

Spouse: Carrie Leona Measures (1904 - 1994).

Schooley Lemmon Morris
Birth:
April 5, 1856
Zanesville
Morgan County, Ohio
Death:
May 19, 1922
Ashley
Washington County, Illinois
Burial:
Unknown
Ashley
Washington County, Illinois

Schooley Lemmon (or Lemon) Morris was born to David and Rachel Ann (James) Morris. In the 1880 census he was listed as a photographer. Later references list him as a Free Will Baptist minister. Morris began to make his mark on Free Will Baptists when he became the editor and publisher of *the Free Will Baptist News,* which he published in Weatherford, Texas, as early as 1910. He also pastored the First Free Will Baptist Church in Weatherford. He was a friend and mentor to the younger Lizzie McAdams, who often referred to him as "father Morris." In 1912 he was an agent for the Southwestern Freewill Baptist General Convention. At the 1912 convention he gave a talk on The Free Will Baptist News.

He continued publishing the News for several years. In 1916 Free Will Baptists in Texas, Oklahoma, and Missouri organized the Cooperative General Association of Free Will Baptists at a meeting at the Philadelphia Church, near Pattonsburg, Missouri. Morris was present and was chosen to preach during one of the evening services. The moderator appointed him to be on a committee to devise reporting forms for the association. Morris also preached at a called session of the association on December 26, 1917, at the Northview Church near Tecumseh, Oklahoma.

The Cooperative General Association at its organizational session voted to purchase the *Free Will Baptist News* from Morris and to name him the editor and publisher. They paid him $350.00 for the News and $913.00 for the printing equipment and other assets, and voted to change the name of the News to the *New Morning Star*. It was printed in Weatherford, Texas, for about a year.

In 1919 Samra Smith, a native of North Carolina, merged his publication, the *Biblical Beacon*, with the Star and became co-editor with Morris. At about the same time Rev. W. C. Austin merged his paper, the *Gospel Pruning Hook*, with the Star, thus three papers became one, with a

much larger circulation. At first the Star was published twice a month, then weekly for a time, and then back to twice a month.

The Cooperative General Association opened Tecumseh College on September 2, 1917.

The *New Morning Star* was moved from Weatherford, Texas, to Tecumseh, Oklahoma. The latest printing equipment was purchased for the Star, such as Linotype, a larger cylinder press, a large job press, a motorized paper cutter, and a mailer. Morris made the move with the Star, and became the first pastor of the Tecumseh College Church, which had been organized earlier in the year. Morris and his wife, Grace I. Morris, were also on the faculty of Tecumseh College. Their salaries were $70.00 per year for each of them.

Morris was widowed twice in his lifetime. In the 1880 census his wife was listed as Josephine Morris, and they had a three month old son, Corral (or Carlos)

W. Morris. On March 4, 1891 he married Belle Adams. In the 1900 census he is listed as having three children: Corral W. age 20; Hallie, E., age 17; and Nellie, age 13. After her death he married Grace Irene Topping on March 24, 1901, in Ashley, Illinois.

Rev. S. L. Morris passed away at the age of 66. In November of 1924 his widow, Grace I. Morris, became the president of Tecumseh College.

Rev Thomas Henry Newsom

Birth:
Aug. 9, 1876
Death:
Jul. 24, 1944
Burial:
Springtown Cemetery
Springtown
Parker County, Texas

Early leader in Texas Freewill Baptist, as chairman, of a committee, in 1929, resisted association with the larger northern group of Baptists, other than in Christian fellowship. (See Hist. of FWB State Associations)

Son of John Randolph Newsom and Mary Dixon, married Mattie Elizabeth Young. Son of John Rabdolph Newsom and Mary Dixon, married Mattie Elizabeth Young (1879 - 1970).

Children: Mary Ruth Newsom Martin (1907 - 1987), Mattie Jewell Newsom (1911 - 2005), Joseph Edward Newsom (1913 - 1992).

Most of his life and ministry was invested in Texas Free Will Baptist churches. In his early years he traveled the state promoting home and foreign missions and gave every month to missions work in Texas. At the time of his death he was the pastor of the new Salem Free Will Baptist Church.

Dr J. D. O'Donnell
Birth:
Apr. 5, 1929
Alabama
Death:
Nov. 29, 2014
Arizona
Burial:
Non-Cemetery Burial
Texas

He was born into a family that gave him a solid foundation in life. He attended Bob Jones University and graduated in 3 years. He came home to Steele, Alabama and was the principal of the Chandler Mountain School for a year. He then went to his first full time pastorate in Columbus, Mississippi. He would go from there to attend the New Orleans Baptist Seminary and would earn his THD. He taught at Welch College in Nashville, Tennessee. He would go from there to be the president of Hillsdale College in Moore, Oklahoma. He would serve as the moderator of the Free Will Baptist denomination for several years. He worked at the Randall House

Oliver Roy Norie, Jr
Birth:
Jul. 24, 1923
Death:
Jul. 19, 1998
Burial:
Crestview Memorial Park,
Wichita Falls,
Wichita County,
Texas

Publications. He would pastor FWB churches in Tennessee, Missouri, and Texas. He would also pastor several Methodist churches in Texas. He retired for the final time from pastoring churches at the age of 78. He is survived by his sons, Dan and Darryl.

JD was a man who loved God, his family and people. He wrote several books for Free Will Baptists including The Deacon Handbook, Faith For Today, Church History and Free Will Baptist Doctrine. He was an educator who had the knack of building a house when he wanted to. His kindness and gentle spirit was the highlight of knowing him. He always had the other person in mind. He had an impact on those who were his students. Earth has lost a great man, but heaven is enriched with his presence!

Judson B Palmer
Birth:
April 25, 1851
Orangeville, Ohio
Death:
1937
Burial:
Galveston Memorial Park
Hitchcock
Galveston County, Texas
Plot: Section B

He attended Hillsdale College in Michigan where he assisted in teaching and graduated from the theological department. He was ordained in May, 1873 with Reverent's A. A. Smith, A. H. Chase and other serving on the Council. He served as a teacher in the Cairo mission for two years and as a state missionary. His pastorates consisted in churches in Michigan, Wisconsin, and Iowa. He was engaged in many revivals where the presence of the spirit was manifest and he baptized over 150 converts. He became the general secretary of the YMCA a Galveston, Texas where he died.

Rev James Luther Payne
Birth:
Dec. 21, 1881
Texas
Death:
Feb. 4, 1965
Houston
Harris County
Texas
Burial:
Forest Park Cemetery
Houston
Harris County
Texas

CASWELL AND SARAH EMLEY (ORRELL) PURSELLEY

Rev Caswell Purselley
Birth:
Nov. 29, 1845
Roane County
Tennessee, USA
Death:
Dec. 17, 1916
Mambrino
Hood County
Texas, USA
Burial:
Nubbin Ridge Cemetery
Mambrino
Hood County, Texas

Married to: Sarah Emily Orrell, on 25 Feb 1866, Zion Hill, Carroll Co, Arkansas

See deed 1849 Hiwasse Dist. Farmer, Preacher (Primitive Baptist). A Descendant who wrote for Hood Co., Tx Genealogical Society, says he was a Freewill Baptist.

Civil War Confederate Arkansas Infantry Caswell Age 16, Capt. Evans' Co., Regiment, McBride's Brigade, AR Infantry. Roll dated at Camp Bragg, AR Feb 15, 1862 to July 31, 1862. Enlisted at Carrollton, by Capt. Evans for 1 year. PVT.
Parents:
James Alpha Purselley (1819 - 1907)
Martha Caroline Osbourne Purselley (1822 - 1870)

Rev James Eldridge Raney
Birth:
Apr. 15, 1861
Allen County, Kentucky
Death:
Jun. 8, 1933
Fall Creek, Hood County,Texas
Burial:
Fall Creek Cemetery
Fall Creek, Hood County,Texas

Rev W B Rhea
Birth:
Feb. 4, 1855
Death:
Jun. 20, 1929
Burial:
Cedar Creek Cemetery
Red River County, Texas

James O. Riggs
Birth: Mar. 17, 1872
Death: Mar. 28, 1954
Burial:
South Park Cemetery
Pearland
Brazoria County
Texas

Spouse:
Gertrude B. Riggs (1887 - 1975)*
Children:
Lida Riggs (1908 - 1953)

Rev R A Roberts
Birth:
Nov. 12, 1865
Death:
Nov. 20, 1930
Burial:
Fall Creek Cemetery
Fall Creek
Hood County, Texas

James Edward Rogers
Birth:
Mar. 11, 1868
Texas
Death:
Oct. 11, 1966
Ennis
Ellis County
Texas
Burial:
Ennis Memorial Cemetery
Ennis
Ellis County
Texas

Son of Austin Rogers and Jane Hooks. Spouse: Sallie Lee Rogers (1876 - 1925) Widowed minister died at 903 S. Preston Street with cerebral hemorrhaging

Information provided by Louis Gipson; James R. Jeter MD
Source: Texas Death Certificate #65261

Marshall I Sanford

Birth:
Nov. 17, 1867
Winn Parish
Louisiana, USA
Death:
Feb. 26, 1940
Dallas
Dallas County
Texas, USA
Burial:
Western Heights Cemetery
Dallas
Dallas County
Texas, USA

Father: William Sanford b NC; mth: Sarah Foster, b NC. wid, age 72 yrs. Ret'd from Nursery Business.

Spouse: Fannie Carter-b. TX

Children:
Sarah Sanford Davidson (1896 - 1926)*
Lee Roy Sanford (1902 - 1974)*
Berta Mae Sanford McCloskey (1905 - 1972)*

Rev James F Scott

Birth:
Feb. 12, 1869
Tennessee, USA
Death:
Jul. 27, 1943
Wichita Falls
Wichita County
Texas, USA
Burial:
Ringgold Cemetery
Ringgold
Montague County
Texas, USA

He was a retired Free Will Baptist minister in the early work in Texas. He attended as a minister, the Southwestern Cooperative Association of FWB in 1912. He was b. Crossville, TN. (see TX Dth cert.)

Father: Henry Taylor Scott
Mother: Zillie Lary
Spouse:
Martha Ellen Whitaker Scott (1868 - 1947)

Rev Thomas A Searcy
Birth:
Nov., 1866
Texas
Death:
1933
Texas
Burial:
Willowhole Cemetery
North Zulch
Madison County, Texas

He was pastor of the First FWB church in Bryan, Texas during the years 1907-1909. He and his wife were also charter members of this church which was organized in 1894 with 14 members.

Robert Edward Lee Sheffield
Birth:
1911
Death:
1984
Burial:
Friendship Cemetery
Kirbyville
Jasper County, Texas

From "The Burial Locations of Free Will Baptist Ministers." DOB/DOD from SSDI and TX Dth Records. He was listed as a son of John B. and Hazel Sheffield, in both 1920-1930 TX Jasper & Walker Co.'s Census'. U.S. Army Veteran of WW II.

Rev J M Smith
Birth:
Dec. 4, 1846
Death:
Aug. 25, 1935
Burial:
Mount Zion Cemetery
Shelby County, Texas

CONFEDERATE VETERAN DIES
·

The Rev. J. M. Smith, 88, of Marshall, Texas, Will Be Buried Today

Marshall, Texas, Aug. 25. (Special) —The Rev. J. M. Smith, 88, retired Methodist pastor and quartermaster general of the Trans-Mississippi division of the United Confederate Veterans, died here today following an illness of about two months.

Funeral services will be held here Monday with burial in the Mt. Zion cemetery near Center.

Reverend Smith was a native Tennessean, being born in Murphysboro, on Dec 4, 1846. He came to Texas with his parents when he was four years of age and settled near Center. Later he moved to Marshall. He was in the ministry during the served the Confederacy during the Civil war, being attached to Perry's brigade. He is survived by his widow

Rev John Abe Smith

BIRTH
7 Apr 1858
Arkansas, USA
DEATH
22 Mar 1939 (aged 80)
Henderson, Rusk County, Texas,
BURIAL
Harmony Hill Cemetery
Henderson, Rusk County, Texas

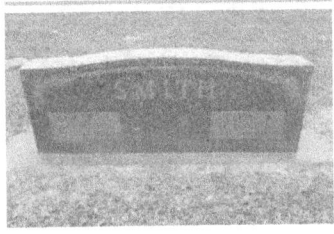

Rev T W Smith

Birth:
May 27, 1881
Death:
Oct. 14, 1954
Burial:
New Prospect Cemetery
New Prospect, Rusk County, Texas
A Free Will Bapt. minister in early
TX church work.
Inscription: "Father"

Rev J W Shults

Birth:
Mar. 11, 1853
Death:
Apr. 3, 1926

Burial:
Buffalo Springs Cemetery
Buffalo Springs
Clay County, Texas

Joseph Wilburn Shults was born in Missouri to W. C. and Melinda Shults, who had migrated west from Kentucky. In the 1860 census, when J. W. was 7, the family was living in Spring Creek Township, Dent County, in South Central Missouri. J. W. married Comilla Frances Bowles (1859-1935), but little else is known about her except that she was born in Texas in June of 1859. In 1900 J. W. and his family were living in Denton County, Texas, on a rented farm with seven children. Their daughter Carrye Dell had been born in Indian Territory in 1894.

In late December of 1913 Shults moved his family to Post Oak, Texas. Less than five months later, on May 1, 1914, he organized the Pleasant Valley Free Will Baptist Church, three miles north of Post Oak and three miles south of Buffalo Springs in Clay County, Texas. The church services were held in the Pleasant Valley School, which was a one room schoolhouse and pastored the church from 1914 to 1919, and again from 1921 to 1924. The church would go on to become one of the better known Free Will Baptist churches in Texas.

Joseph and "Fannie" had seven children: George L., Maggie B., Effie B., John P., Carrye Dell, Clyde A, and William P. Carrye Dell married Rev. Tiff Covington who twice pastored the church Brother Shults had started (1928-1949; 1967-1980). Tiff had been converted at the Pleasant Valley Church when Brother Shults was preaching a revival in August of 1916. Tiff would go on to become a legend in North Central Texas. In 1936 the Pleasant Valley Church built a new sanctuary one mile north of Pleasant Valley. The new church was on higher ground than at its previous location in the valley and its name was changed to the Pleasant Mound Free Will Baptist Church, affectionately known in the community as the Rock Church, because it was constructed of local field stones. He and Fannie are buried in the Buffalo Springs Cemetery in Texas.

Lucy Gressett is listed in the 1909 and 1911 Free Will Baptist Registers as being a member of the Spring Hill Free Will Baptist Church, the Plainview Quarterly Meeting, and the Southwestern Free Will Baptist General Convention. She was residing in Iola at the time. Spouse:Ruben Snook (1874 - 1959)

Clarice Lucinda Gressett Snook
Birth:
Aug. 7, 1877
Louisiana, USA
Death:
Sep. 7, 1933
Houston
Harris County
Texas
Burial:
Concord Cemetery
Iola
,Grimes County,
Texas

Photo Courtesy of: Landry Morren ~ Floydada, TX

Nicholas Burkhardt Stanley
Birth:
Mar. 7, 1858
Howard County
Missouri, USA
Death:

May 16, 1941
Floydada
Floyd County
Texas, USA
Burial:
Floydada Cemetery
Floydada
Floyd County, Texas, USA
Plot: North, Section 2, Row 1,
Space 23

Newton Willis Stout
Birth:
Jan. 7, 1895
Normangee
Leon County
Texas, USA
Death:
Nov. 19, 1984
Harris County
Texas, USA
Burial:
Glenwood Cemetery
Houston
Harris County
Texas, USA
Plot: Section I, Lot 119

Son of Delano Stout and Frances "Fannie" Davies.
FW Bapt.Minister in Texas.
Spouse:
Myrtle Monroe Williams Stout (1901 - 1973)
Children:
Harold N. Stout (1925 - 1944)*

Angus McAllister Stewart
Birth:
Aug. 25, 1853
Death:
Sep. 17, 1913
Burial:
Odd Fellows Cemetery
Carthage
Panola County,Texas

In 1878 a number of churches in Panola County entered into an organization which became known as the Texas Association. He was very instrumental in to organize associations as well as local churches.

He and his wife we among the 14 charter members of the Bryan First FWB church and its first pastor.

During his ministry the church began to grow and he owned and operated The Bryan Academic and Collegiate Institute, which was a grade school. This school filled a unique place in the early history of Bryan and the church.

Lula & Thomas Strain

Thomas Albert Strain, Jr
Birth:
Nov. 25, 1885
Death:
Nov. 16, 1971
Seadrift
Calhoun County
Texas, USA
Burial:
Seadrift Cemetery
Seadrift
Calhoun County,
Texas
Plot: A-222-5
WEDDED 65 YEARS
Spouse: Lula Mae Bone Strain
(1888 - 1977)

John Swanwick
Birth:
Jun. 13, 1870
Bradley
Kankakee County, Illinois
Death:
Aug. 2, 1941
Houston,Harris County, Texas
Burial:
Bryan City Cemetery
Bryan (Brazos County)
Brazos County, Texas
Plot: Block 4 Lot 95/C

Early Texas minister.

Milton L Sutton
Birth:
Jan. 25, 1899
Louisiana
Death:
Nov. 1, 1980
Wichita Falls,
Wichita County,
Texas
Burial:
Buffalo Springs Cemetery,
Buffalo Springs,
Clay County, Texas

He was an ordained pastor and leader in the Texas church. He pastored at Ft. Worth for years and was a popular and able leader in Texas and the national.

Rev Isaac G. Swearingen
Birth:
Jan. 14, 1854
Death:
Jan. 3, 1919
Burial:
Swearingen Cemetery
Warren
Tyler County,Texas

Rev Lemuel Geren Sweat
BIRTH
15 Nov 1919
Pitkin, Vernon Parish, Louisiana,
DEATH
4 Sep 1982 (aged 62)
Groves,
Jefferson County,
Texas,
BURIAL
Beech Creek Baptist Cemetery
Spurger,
Tyler County,
Texas

Rev John Julian Tatum
Birth:
May 22, 1863
Steeleville
Randolph County, Illinois
Death:
Mar. 10, 1931
Bryan
Brazos County, Texas
Burial:
Bryan City Cemetery
Bryan
Brazos County, Texas

He received his theological education at Hillsdale College in Michigan. He was ordained in 1889 in his home church in Steeleville. On June 22, 1886, he married Hettie K. Mason in Pinkneyville, Illinois. Together Rev. and Mrs. Tatum served churches in Illinois, Indiana, and Iowa, until they accepted the call to the Bryan Free Will Baptist Church in 1905, a church he pastored three times, 1905-07, 1910-13, 1918-19. In 1914 he served as agent,

promotional man, of the Southwestern Convention of Freewill Baptists and General Conference of Free Baptists, though his salary was paid exclusively by the General Conference. At the first annual session of the Texas State Association of Free Will Baptists, held October 8-9, 1915, at Bradley, Texas, Rev. Tatum was appointed by moderator E. L. Hill to serve on a committee to draft the first by-laws and constitution for the state association. He served on the committee with Rev. W. E. Dearmore and Rev. Charles C. Wheeler, two other men of able leadership capacity. Over the years he served on numerous committees and boards, displaying considerable literary skills and organizational abilities, reflecting the excellent training he had received at Hillsdale College in Michigan. From 1918 on the Tatum family lived in Bryan until their deaths. The Bryan area was a stronghold for Free Will Baptists in the first half of the twentieth century.

As Field Secretary of the Southwest for the Free Will Baptist denomination, serving Texas, Oklahoma, Arkansas, Missouri, Kansas, and Nebraska.

Old church history says, "Rev. J. J. Tatum, was elected president in 1912, of the Southwestern Freewill Baptist General Convention which included Okla., Missouri, as well as Texas. He was closly allied with the northern FWB.

Township 6, with six children. *"First Hundred Years of Oklahoma Free Will Baptist,"* pub. 2009, states that in Rev. J.M. Robert's diary, "O.J. Tailor (sic), was in Indian Territory in 1894, and preached with Rev. J. M. Roberts. In meeting minutes of Sept. 1, 1894, organization of churches in Indian Territory, 'Rev. O. J. Taylor, was elected ass't moderator' of their group. Where he was ordained and where his ministry took him is not known. It's possible he was ordained in Arkansas after they moved there. His occupation was always listed as "farmer" as most of the old pioneer ministers were, as they received precious little money for their ministerial labor.

Obediah J. Taylor
Birth:
Feb. 14, 1851
Anderson County,
South Carolina
Death:
Feb. 14, 1939
Smith County, Texas,
Burial:
Hopewell Cemetery,
Swan, Smith County, Texas

His father died in 1864, in Franklin, Tennessee, Civil War, which left his mother a widow. She died about 1880 when they were in Mountain Home, Logan Co. Arkansas. After this is when he probably migrated to Indian Territory in eastern Oklahoma, for they were in the Chickasaw Nation census of 1900,

Harold R Teague
Birth:
Nov. 30, 1937
Newport
Cocke County, Tennessee
Death:
Jan. 2, 2012
Burial:
Rusk County Memorial Gardens
Henderson
Rusk County, Texas

He attended Free Will Baptist Bible College in Nashville, Tennessee. He was a pastor and began his career preaching in Springfield, Tennessee in 1959. He then pastored Harris Memorial Freewill Baptist Church in Greeneville, Tennessee, First Freewill Baptist Church in Henderson, Texas,

Longview Freewill Baptist Mission in Longview, Texas, Union Arbor Freewill Baptist in Beckville, Texas and returned again to First Free Will Baptist Church in Henderson where he retired in July 2007. Throughout his career, he held many positions of leadership in the Free Will Baptist Denomination at the district, state, and national level. He was honored as Who's Who in American Religion and touched many lives throughout his ministry career. He also worked for many years on the campuses of the schools for Pine Tree ISD. He was a member of the Lion's Club of Henderson, Texas. He was an incredible husband, father, grandfather, friend and pastor, but most of all he was a devoted follower of Jesus Christ.

Charles B. Thompson
Birth:
Mar. 17, 1890

Death:
Sep. 2, 1977
Burial:
Bryan City Cemetery
Bryan
Brazos County, Texas
Plot: Block 21

PVT US Army World War II. Spouse: Annie Lawless Thompson (1897 – 1988).

Rev Elbert J. Vaughn
Birth:
Apr. 8, 1889
Death:
Nov. 23, 1974
Burial:
Bright Light Cemetery
Bryan (Brazos County)
Brazos County, Texas

Emmett Thomas Vestal, Jr
Birth
11 Nov 1926
Death
11 Feb 1989
Burial
Rosewood Cemetery
Humble, Harris County, Texas

Phila Mae Montgomery Vestal
Birth
28 Aug 1926
Athens,
Henderson County, Texas,
Death
2 Jan 2003
Vidor,
Orange County, Texas
Burial
Rosewood Funeral Home
Cemetery
Humble, Harris County, Texas,

Rev Bishop Abraham Wainwright
BIRTH
21 Jul 1889
DEATH
5 May 1947 (aged 57)
BURIAL
Grange Hall Cemetery
Marshall, Harrison County, Texas

He was a minister in the TX State Association in the 1920's and 1930's. He was elected Assistant moderator in 1926.

Elihu Nelson Waldrep
Birth:
Apr. 1, 1859
Moscow
Polk County
Texas, USA
Death:
Oct. 11, 1930
Texas, USA
Burial:
Midtown Cemetery
Saratoga
Hardin County
Texas

Burrell Green Walker
BIRTH
13 May 1859
Texas, USA
DEATH
29 Jan 1925 (aged 65)
Texas, USA
BURIAL
Authon Cemetery
Authon, Parker County, Texas

Rev James M. Walker
BIRTH
10 Aug 1861
Somervell County, Texas, USA
DEATH
8 Mar 1942 (aged 80)
Weatherford, Parker County, Texas, USA
BURIAL
East Greenwood Cemetery
Weatherford, Parker County, Texas

James M. Walker was the son of James Milton Walker and Sarah Elizabeth Sewell. She was remarried by 1880 to G. B. King (b. 1831, Georgia) who died before 1900. His mother was born 1834 in Alabama and may have died in Parker County; she was living with her son, Rev. James M., in 1900 in Parker County.

Rev. James M. Walker married Sarah Jane Brown in Parker County on 14 Aug 1878. Sarah was born 2 Aug 1861 in Weatherford, Texas and died 9 Mar 1907. James and Sarah had seven children, four sons and three daughters.

In addition to being a Free Will Baptist minister, James owned and operated a cafe in Weatherford.

After Sarah's death, James married Verda E. Smith who was thirty-two years younger than he. James and Verda had three children: Fritz Morris, Mattie Elizabeth and Jimmie Sue.

James pastored the First Free Will Baptist (FWB) Church in Weatherford from 1902-1904, and again from October 1915-December 1918. Verda pastored the same church from August 1940 to September 1942. She assisted her husband while he pastored the New Hope FWB Church in Parker County, Texas, and did the same while he pastored a church in Adams, Nebraska, near Lincoln.

They worked together in a number of ministry efforts. They were elected as evangelists by the Southwestern FWB Convention in 1914. Using a large tent owned by the convention, they preached evangelistic meetings far and wide, much the same way Lizzie McAdams used a tent for her campaigns -- many of which resulted in the establishment of Free Will Baptist churches.

James and Verda both worked with Rev. S.L. Morris, publisher and editor of the "Free Will Baptist News" and then "The New Morning Star," both published in Weatherford, until "The New Morning Star" moved to Tecumseh, OK, circa 1916. They worked together in preaching revival meetings in FWB churches as well.

As of 2014 James and Verda still have descendants who are active in the First FWB Church in Weatherford. One of them, Deacon Morris Brandon, a grandson, was named after Rev. S. L. Morris, who was so helpful to young ministers, such as Verda Smith Walker, Lizzie Lawless McAdams and countless others.

Rev James Milton Walker
Birth:
Aug. 10, 1861
Johnson County, Texas
Death:
Mar. 8, 1942
Weatherford
Parker County, Texas

Burial:
East Greenwood Cemetery
Weatherford
Parker County, Texas

He married Sarah Jane Brown on August 14, 1878. Sarah was born in Weatherford, Texas, August 2, 1861. James and Sarah had seven children, four sons and three daughters. Sarah passed away on March 9, 1907. In addition to being a Free Will Baptist minister, James owned and operated a café in Weatherford.

After Sarah's death James married Verda E. Smith, who had been born on August 19, 1893, Grimes County, Texas, and who was thirty-two years younger than he. James and Verda had three children: Fritz Morris, 1913; Mattie Elizabeth, 1914; and Jimmie Sue, 1925.

James pastored the First Free Will Baptist Church in Weatherford twice, from 1902 to 1904, and from October 1915 to December of 1918. Verda pastored it from August of 1940 to September of 1942. She assisted him while he pastored the New Hope Free Will Baptist Church in Parker County, Texas, and did the same while he pastored a church in Adams, Nebraska, near Lincoln. They worked together in a number of ministry efforts. They were elected as evangelists by the Southwestern Free Will Baptist Convention in 1914. Using a large tent owned by the convention, they preached evangelistic meetings far and wide, much the same way Lizzie McAdams used a tent for her campaigns, many of which resulted in the establishment of Free Will Baptist churches. James and Verda both worked with Rev. S. L. Morris, publisher and editor of the *Free Will Baptist News* and then *The New Morning Star,* both published in Weatherford, until *The New Morning Star* was moved to Tecumseh, Oklahoma, circa 1916. They worked together in preaching revival meetings in Free Will Baptist churches, as well.

As of 2014 James and Verda still have descendants who are active in the First Free Will Baptist Church in Weatherford. One of them, Deacon Morris Brandon, a grandson, was named after Rev. S. L. Morris, who was so helpful to young ministers, such as Verda Smith Walker, Lizzie Lawless McAdams, and countless others.

Verda Walker
Birth:
Aug. 19, 1893
Death:
Apr. 8, 1968
Burial:
East Greenwood Cemetery
Weatherford
Parker County, Texas

Verda was ordained to the gospel ministry at the New Hope Free Will Baptist Church on March 31, 1912, by the West Fork District Association. Among the men who signed her ordination certificate were Rev. James Milton Walker, who would later become her husband, and Rev. S. L. Morris.

It was Verda Smith Walker who performed the wedding ceremony for Rev. Lizzie Lawless and Rev. H. M. McAdams. Verda and Lizzie McAdams were close friends until Lizzie passed away in 1964.

James passed away on March 8, 1942 and Verda joined him on April 8, 1968. They are buried beside each other in the East Greenwood Cemetery in Weatherford, Parker County, Texas.

Forest Bernice "Buddy" Welch
BIRTH
1 Jun 1926
DEATH
28 Apr 1970 (aged 43)
BURIAL
Miller Cemetery
Carthage, Panola County, Texas

He was a minister and pastor in Texas dying at an early age.

Alfred Washington West
BIRTH
4 Feb 1863
Texas, USA
DEATH
6 Oct 1956 (aged 93)
Texas, USA
BURIAL
Zion Hill Cemetery
Jasper, Jasper County, Texas

C. C. Wheeler
Birth:
Jan. 28, 1886
Death:
Jan. 14, 1918
Burial:
Bryan City Cemetery
Bryan (Brazos County)
Brazos County, Texas
Plot: Block 5 Lot 09/J

He received his theological training at Westminister College in Tehuascana, Texas. He served the Bryan First FWB church from 1913-15 and again from 1917-1918. He also held pastorates at Geneva, and Sutton, Nebraska, and in North Zulch, Kurren, Wellborn, Cross, Bright Light and Keith,Texas.

Being an educated man, Wheeler was appointed to a committee to draft the first constitution of the Texas State Association at its initial session in 1915 at Bradley, Texas. He served along with Rev. J. J. Tatum and Rev. W. E. Dearmore, two other men of unusual abilities.

Brother Wheeler married Maude Ellie Wheeler (1887-1963) and they had six children: Ruby, Ewell, Charles, Imaree, Mohnike, and Florence.

Wheeler's ministry was brought to an early end when he died in a train wreck on January 14, 1918, at the age of 31 years. Rev. J. J. Tatum signed his death certificate.

Rev Charles Booth Whiteley
Birth:
Apr. 26, 1800
Virginia
Death:
Apr. 27, 1875
Bell County,Texas
Burial:
Resthaven Cemetery
Belton, Bell County,Texas

Charles Booth Whitely, was the son of Joseph and Sarah (Stapleton) Whitely. Charles had two brothers, (among others), Samuel and Isaac Whitely, who all left Virginia, travelled through Tennessee, and on to Northwestern Arkansas, into Marion, then Madison Co. Charles B. was a United Baptist minister, and was the first of the brothers to settle in the newly opened Arkansas territory, and soon after his arrival, he established the Union United Baptist Church in Marion Co. at least by 1838. Goodspeed, in his History of Northwestern AR, mentions these brothers and their missionary work. These United Baptists were no strangers to the Separatist or Free Will history in Kentucky, but were a part of it.

C.B. Whitely and others left Middle Tennessee about 1835, along with the Isaac Boren, and Joel Plumley, for a a new beginning in Arkansas after a break with the Primitive Baptists over foreordination and free salvation issues. He along with the Plumley family and others organized a United church in the Plumley home in July 1838. Other churches were soon organized and the Union Association of United Baptist was formerly organized. (This info from old Association Minutes). This Union Ass'n was closely associated with the FreeWill Baptist throughout the ninetenth century. The Ass'n reported to the New England General Conference as early as 1883. (From William F. Davidson's History of FWB, 1727-1984, pub. 1985, Randall House Publications).

Rev. Charles B. and wife Sarah, were still in Carroll, at Prairie in 1860, (info below says they removed to Texas in 1861 or 1862)-- and certainly before 1870 he was in Bell Co. TX census. He wrote to his 'beloved daughters' in 1866, from Texas, saying his goodbyes, as he had typhoid fever and it looked to him as though he would not recover. He did get medical treatment, and at the end of the letter, it stated that he thought he would recover. And he did.

CHARLES BOOTH WHITELEY

The following is from the "Whitely Family Genealogy:"

"Charles Booth Whiteley was a Baptist minister, man of public spirit. Fair ability as a speaker, with character worthy of his calling. he was active in the support of free schools." (History of Northwest Arkansas).

He was one of the first men to be in the tanning business, known to be very strict. but held in the greatest respect by children, grandchildren, and in-laws. He had a store at one time in Arkansas. He was a Free-will Baptist preacher, and never charged for marriages or funerals. He went to Texas in the fall of 1861 or spring of 1862.

Richard V Whitaker
Birth: Sep. 12, 1866
Death: Sep. 16, 1944
Burial:
Mount Olivet Cemetery
Fort Worth
Tarrant County
Texas, USA
Plot: Plaza Garden

He married Mary Ann Coffey in in Hopkins County, Texas, on January 17, 1872.

Jasper Charles Withers, Sr
Birth:
Jan. 21, 1854
Indiana
Death:
Aug. 24, 1911
Comanche
Comanche County, Texas
Burial:
Oakwood Cemetery
Comanche
Comanche County, Texas

W. T. Wood
Birth:
Apr. 18, 1845
Death:
Feb. 6, 1910
Burial:
Bright Light Cemetery
Bryan, Brazos County, Texas
He was a minister in the Brazos County Association which was organized by the Rev. T.H. Adams with the assistance of Rev. A.M. Stewart in the late 1800s

Rev Wendell Keith Woody
Birth:
Aug. 26, 1940
Mountain Home, Ark.,
Death:
Jul. 20, 2016
Texas
Burial:
Peaceful Gardens Memorial Park
Woodrow
Lubbock County, Texas

Wendell Keith was born to Arthur and Lyddie Woody. He married Neva Mowery on Dec. 24, 1959, in Levelland, Texas.

Keith Woody served as the pastor of eight different churches over the span of four decades in the ministry. He was a national leader in the Free Will Baptist Denomination. He was a loving husband, father, and grandfather.

There's nothing certain in a man's life except this:

That he must lose it.